FISH AND SEA CREATURES

COLORING BOOK

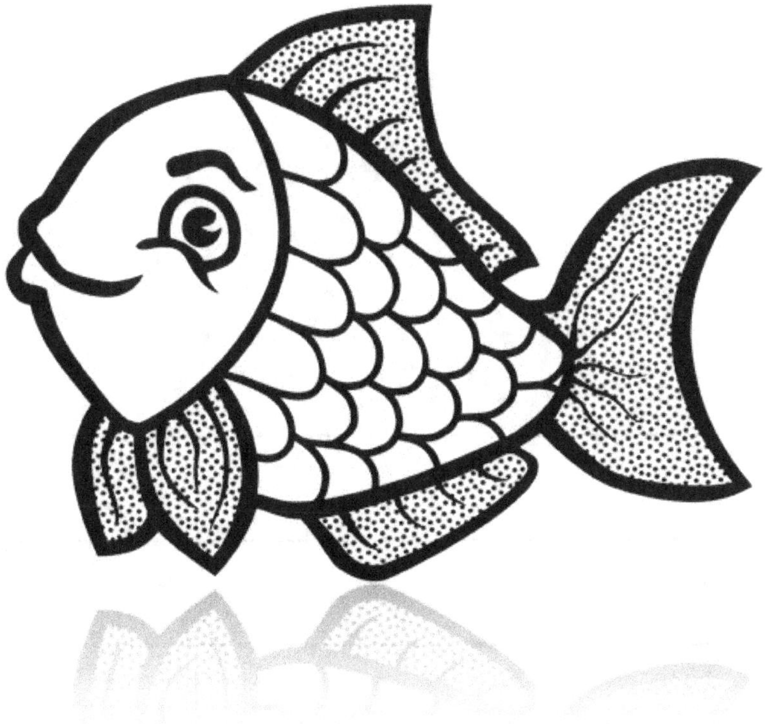

AQUATIC AND UNDERWATER ANIMALS

COLORING BOOK FOR KIDS AND ADULTS

THIS FISH COLORING BOOK BELONGS TO:

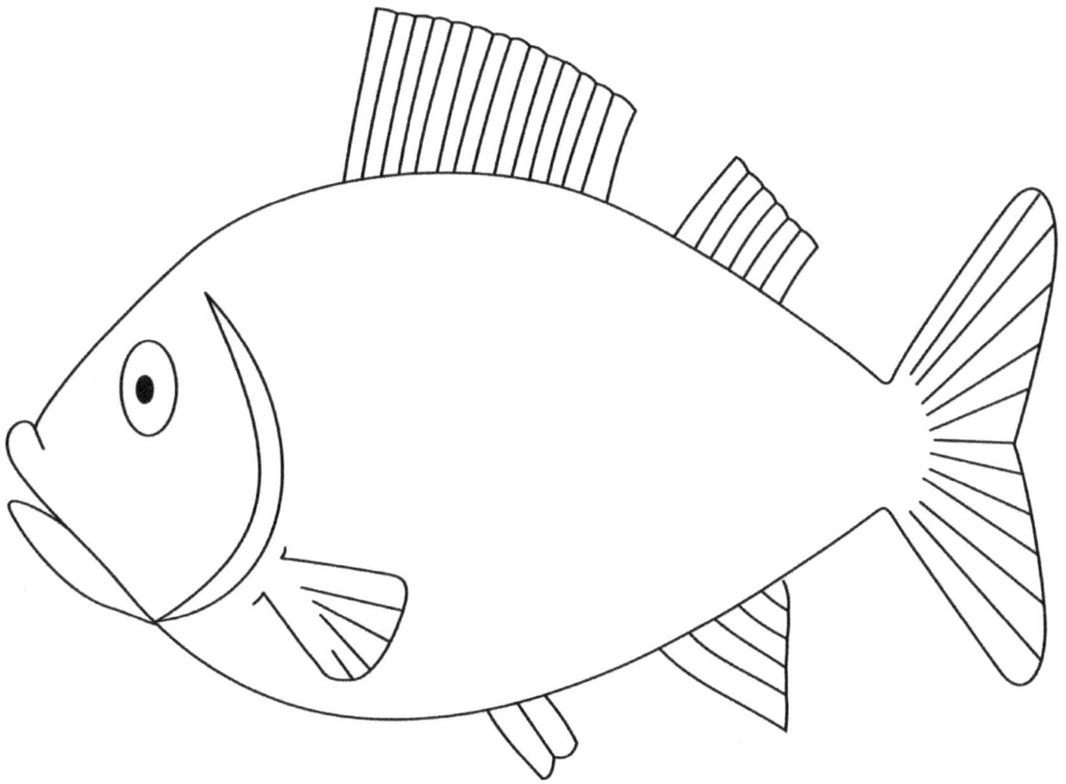

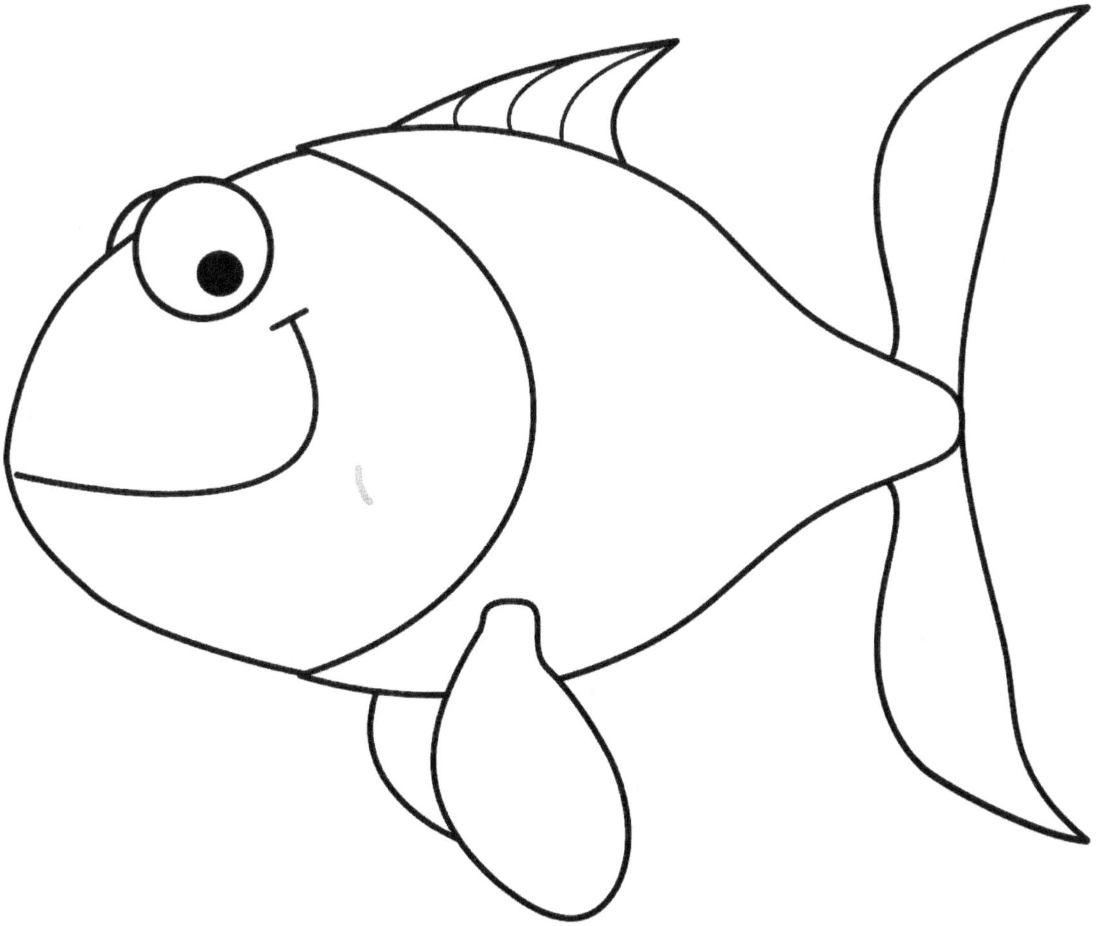

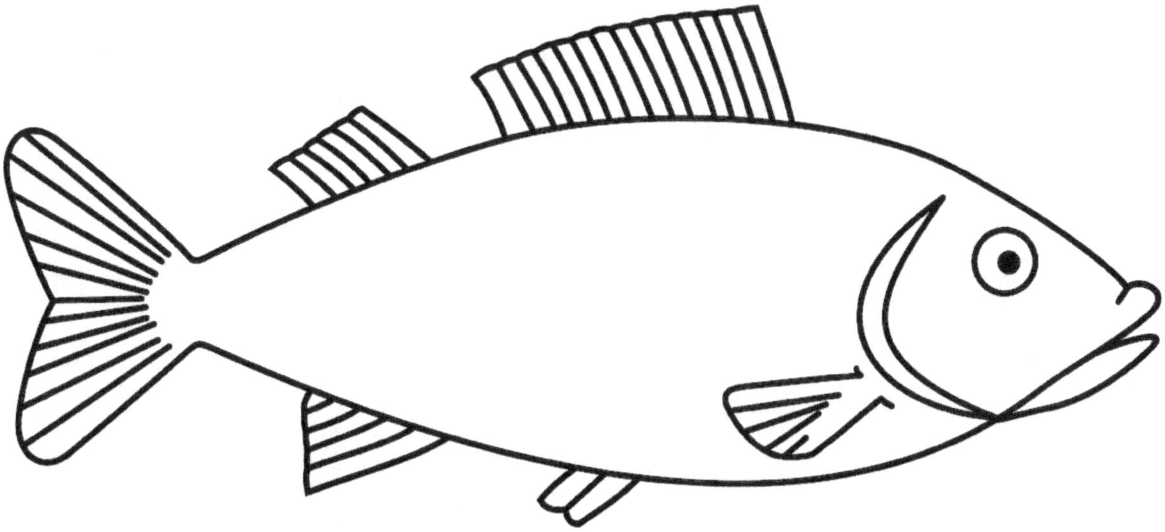

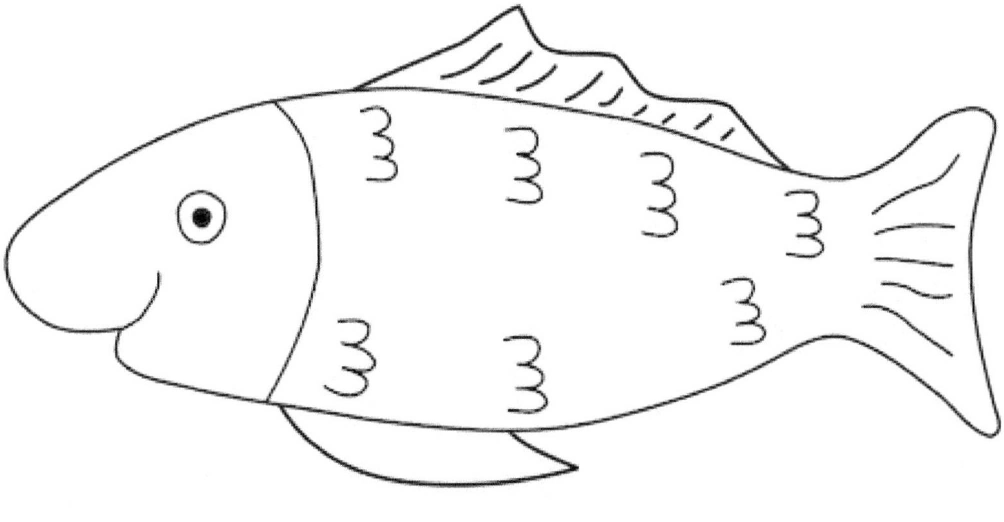

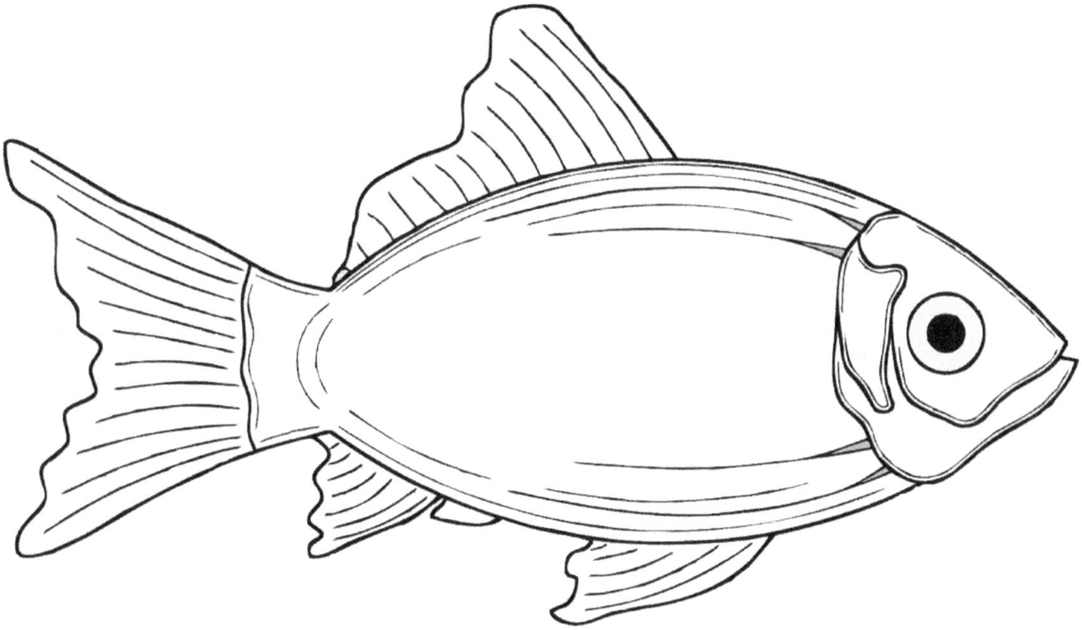

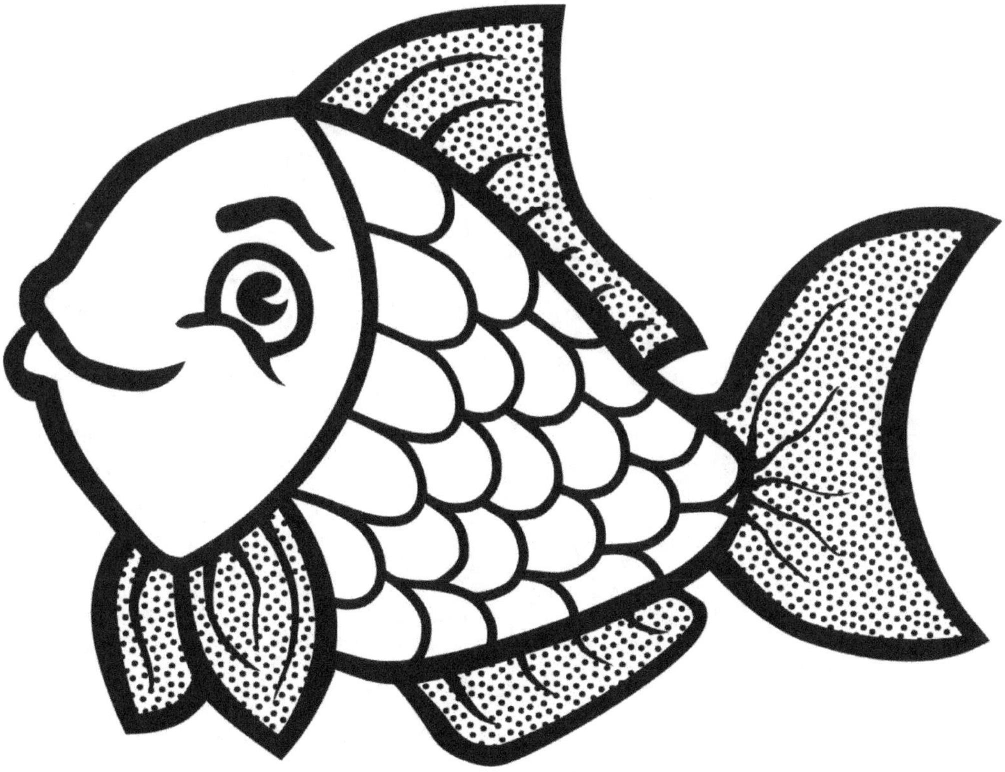

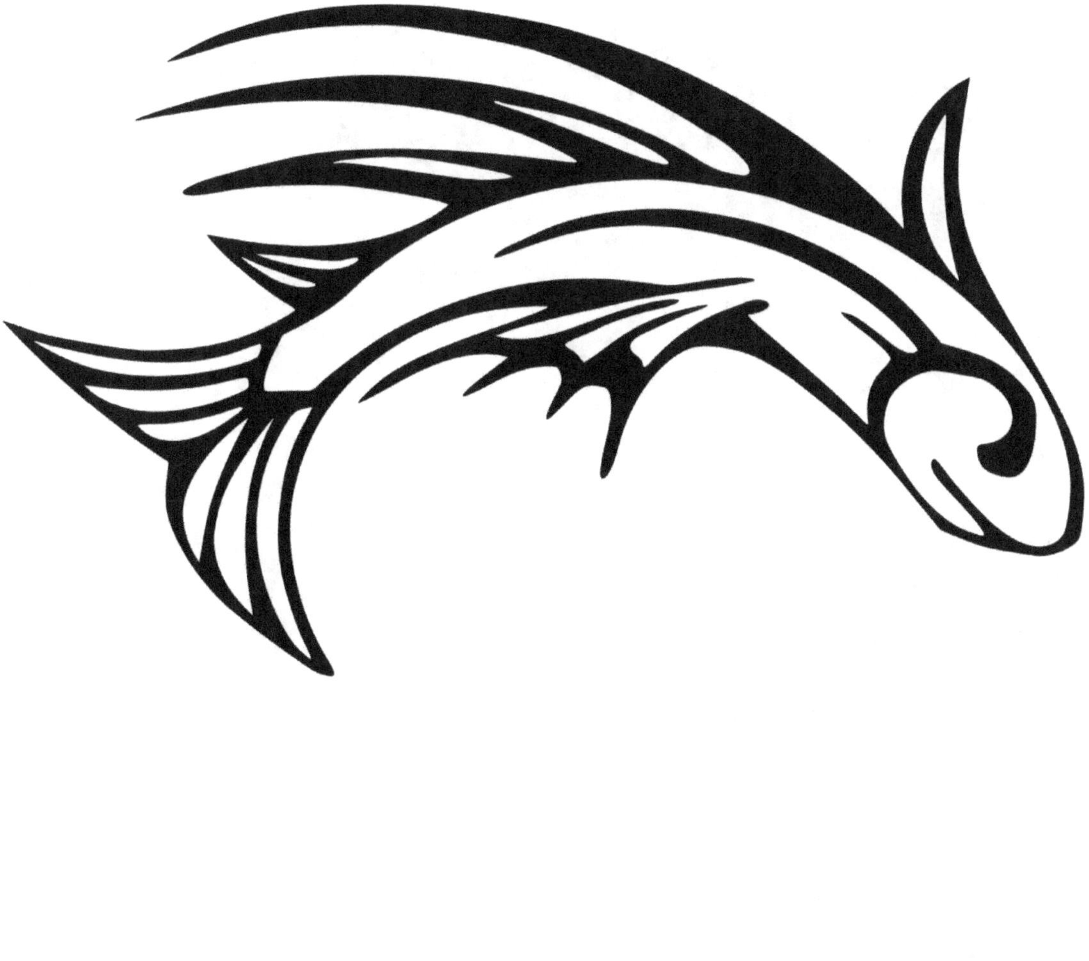

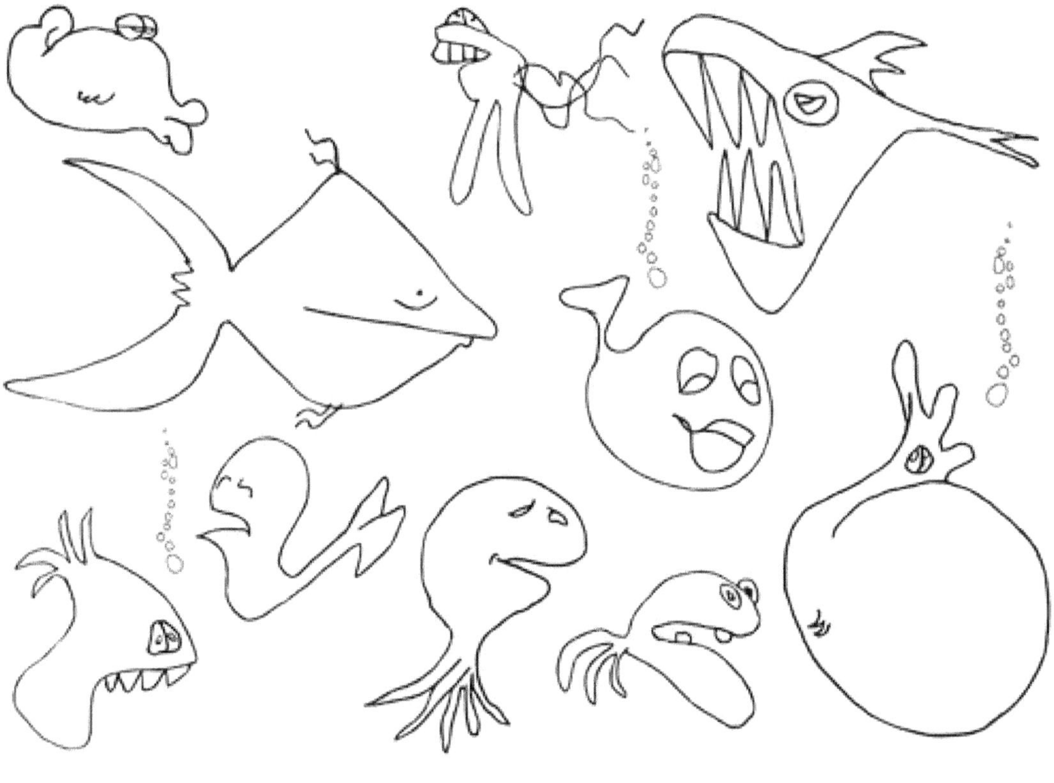

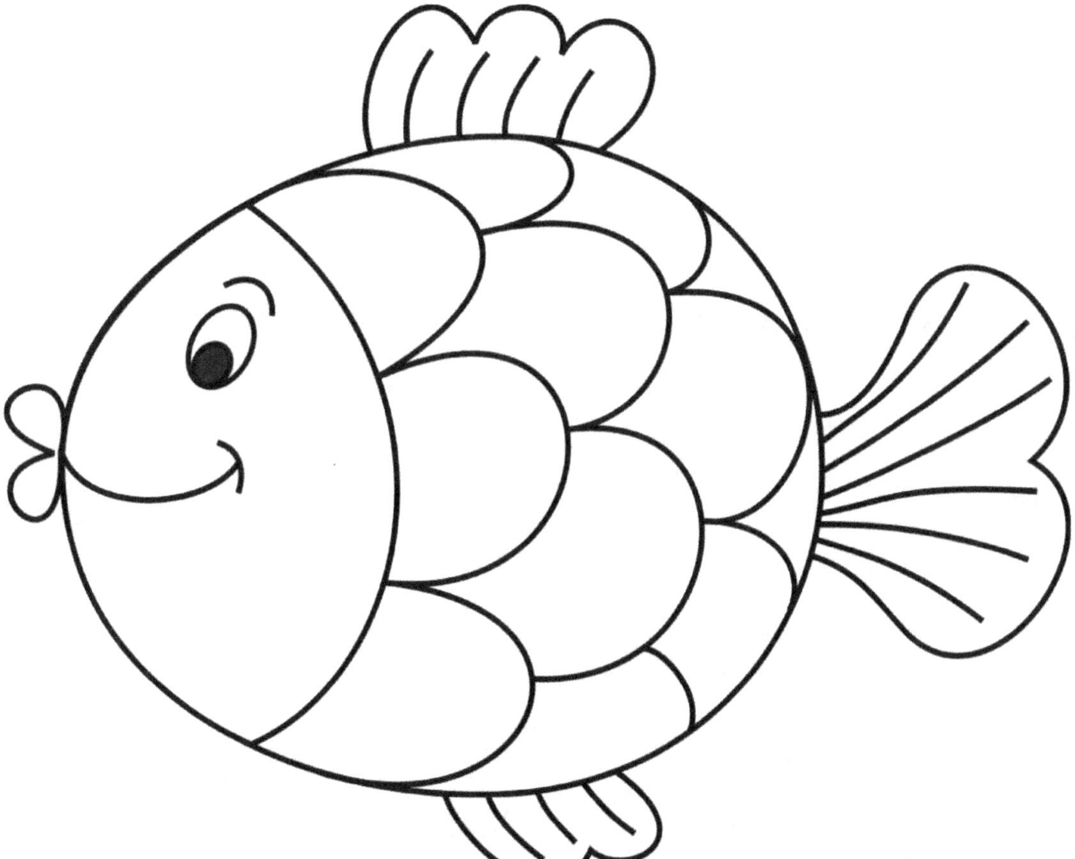

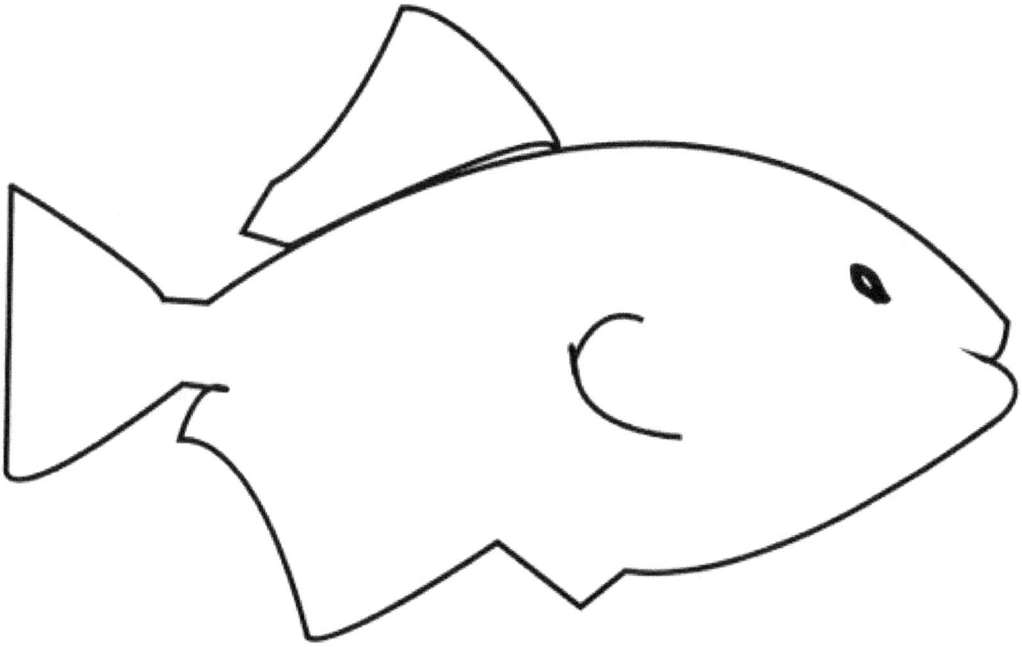

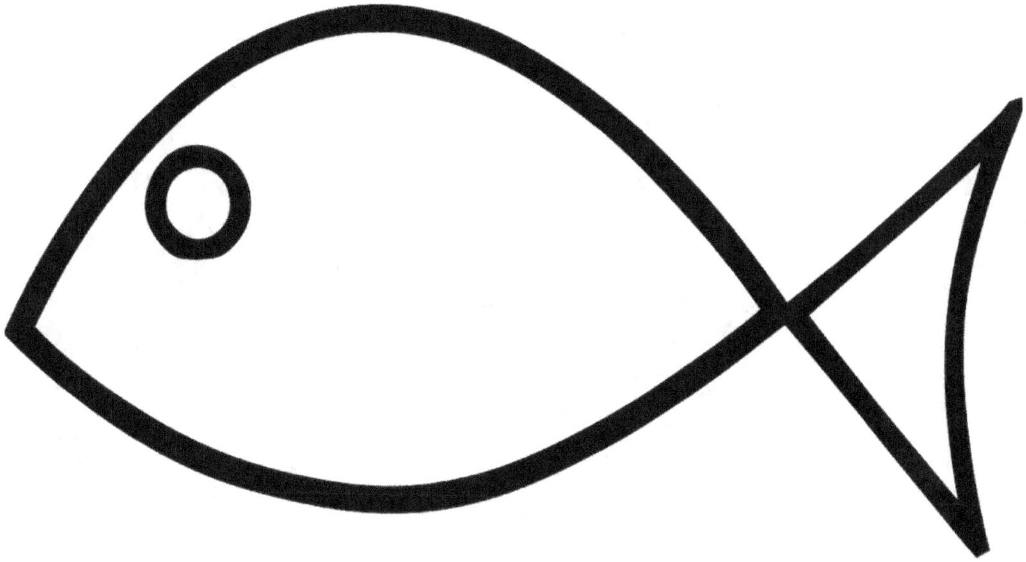

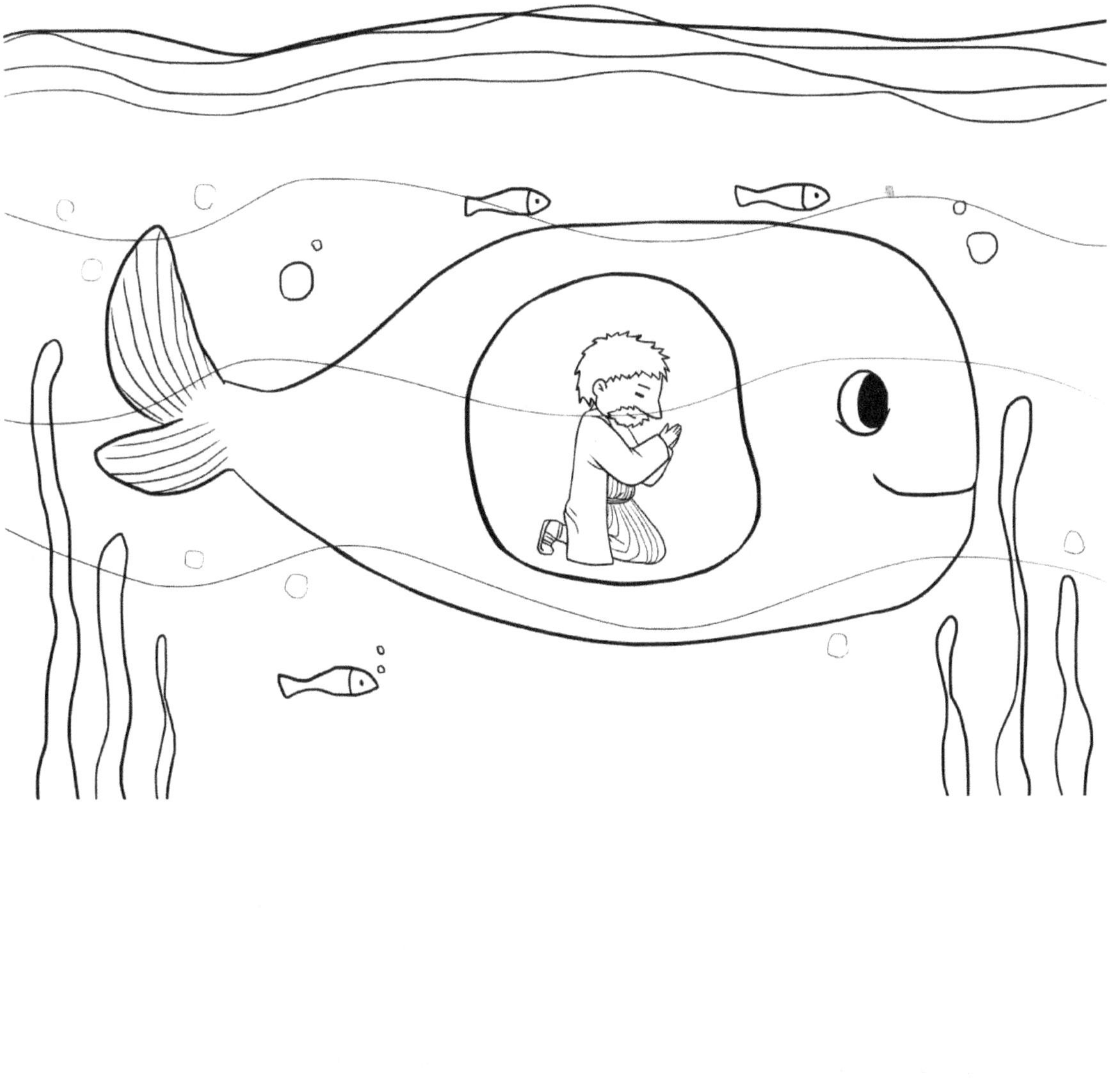

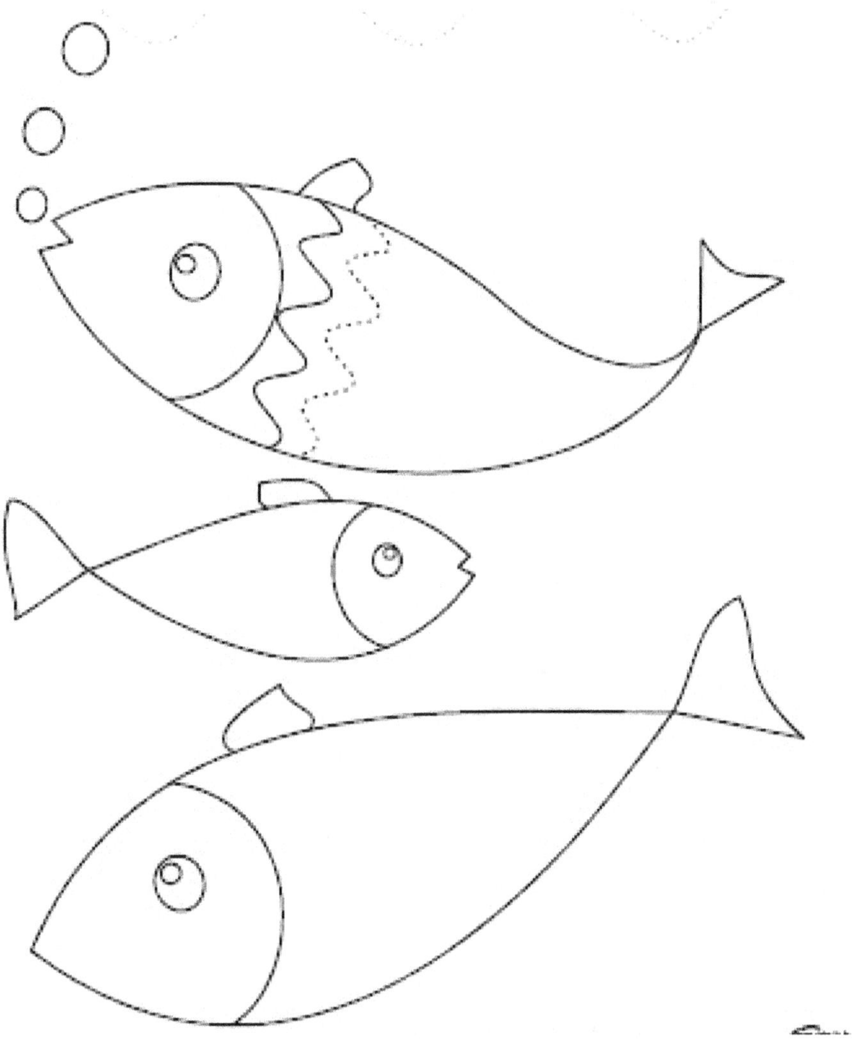

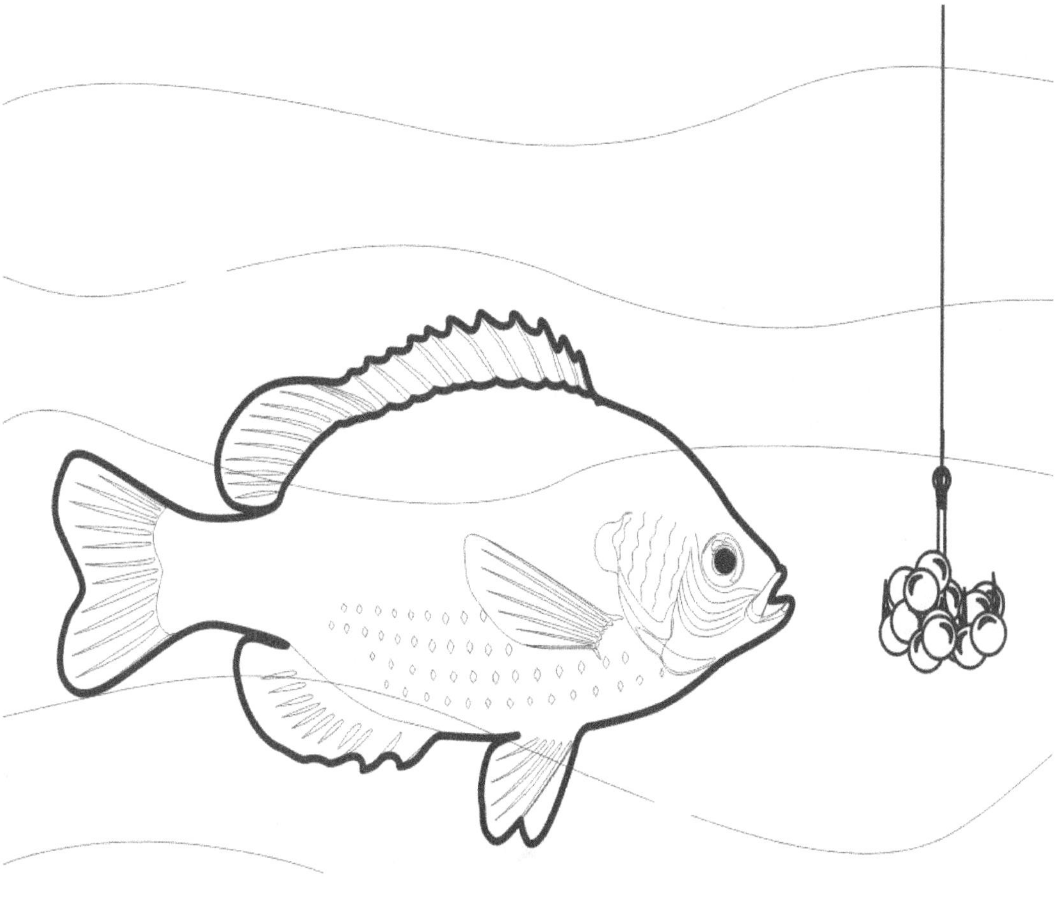

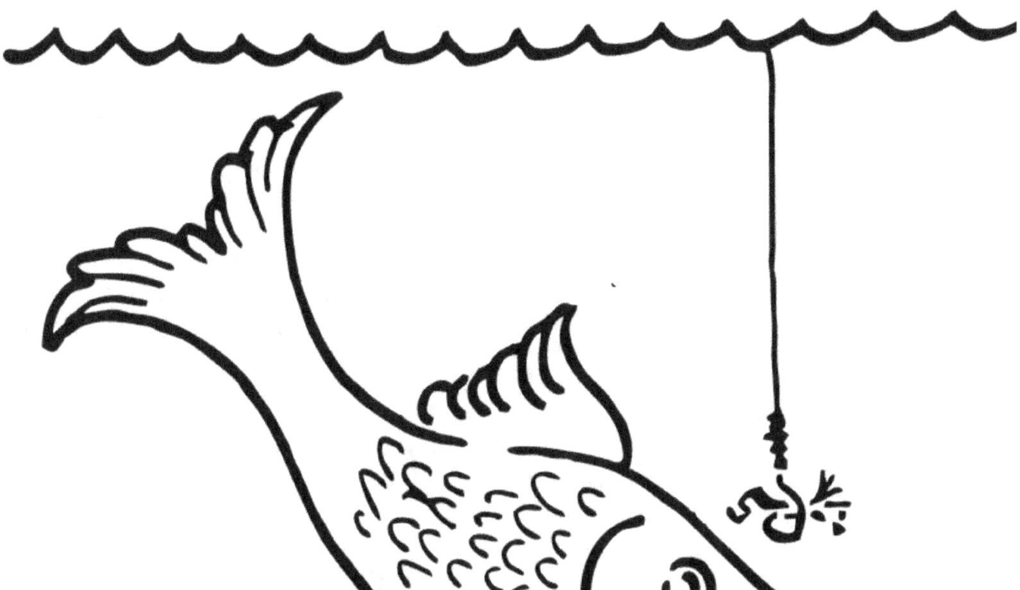

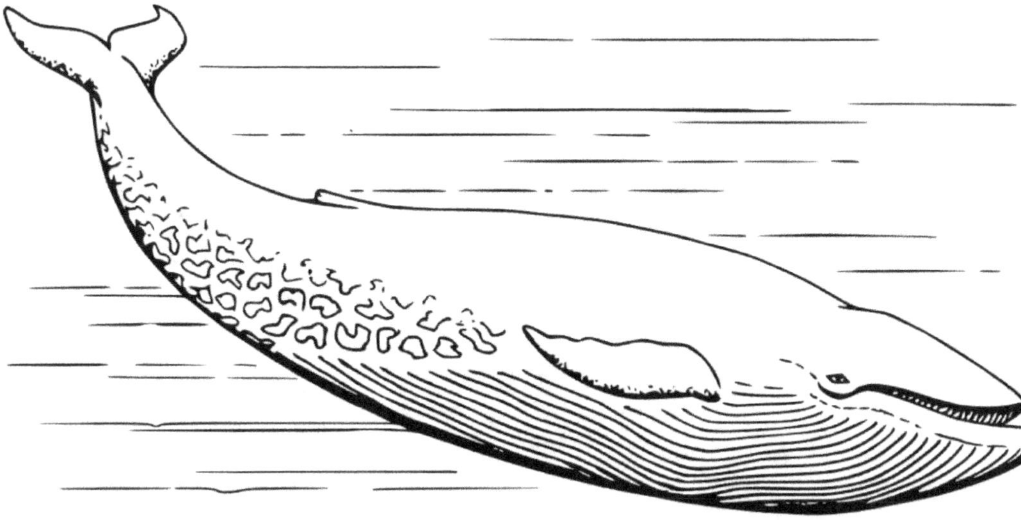

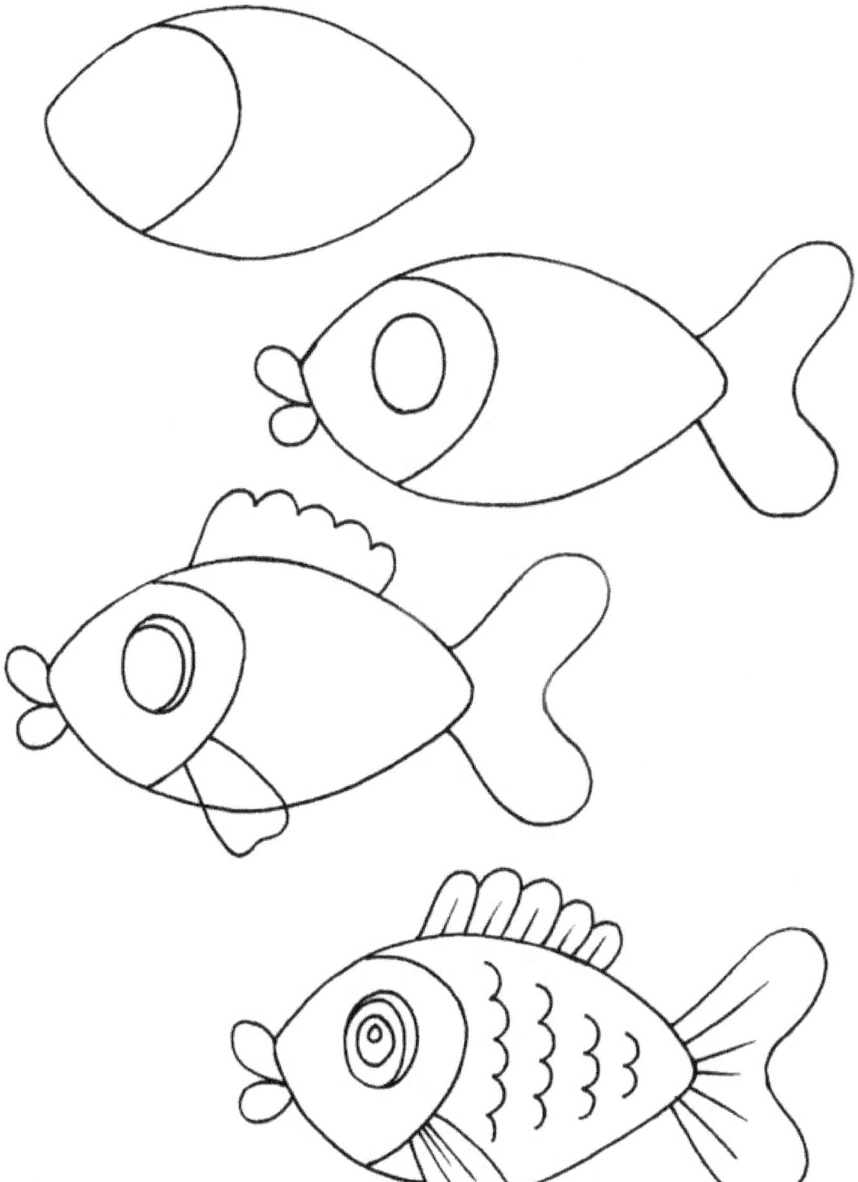

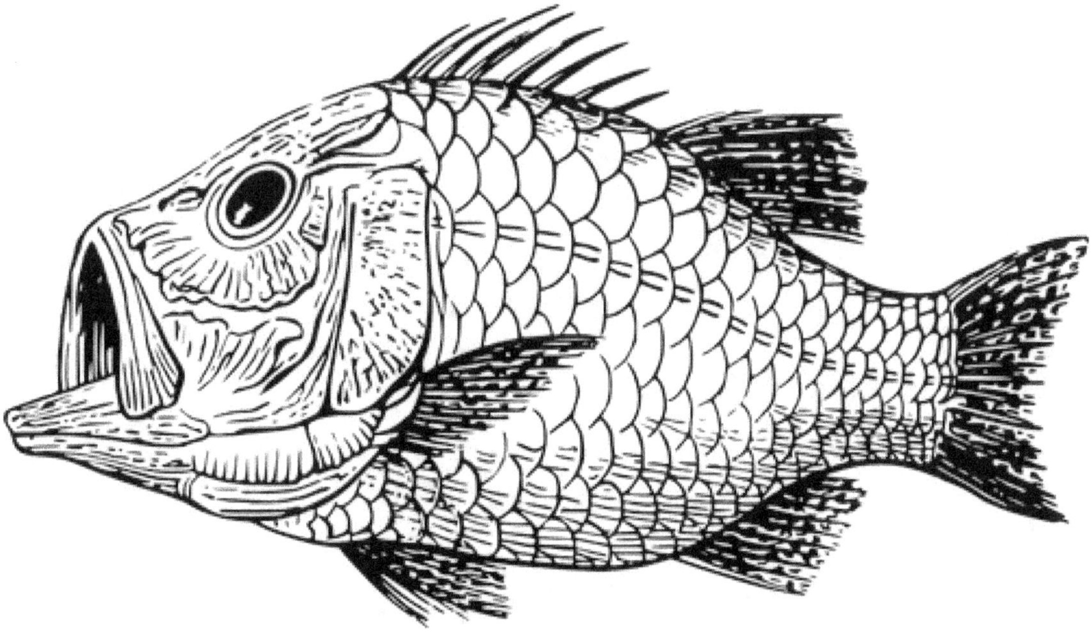

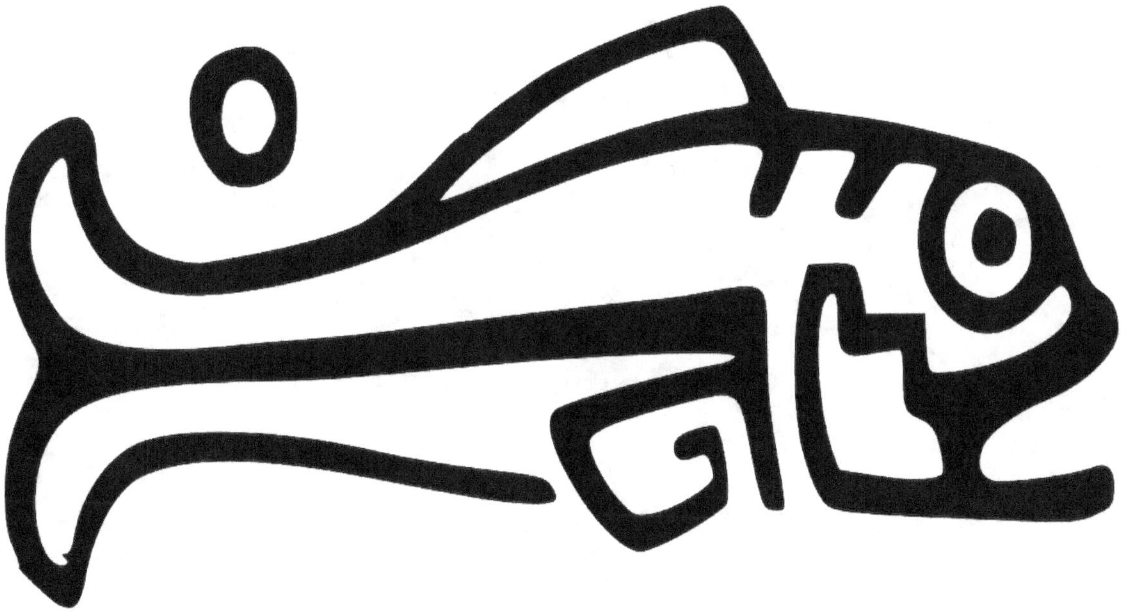

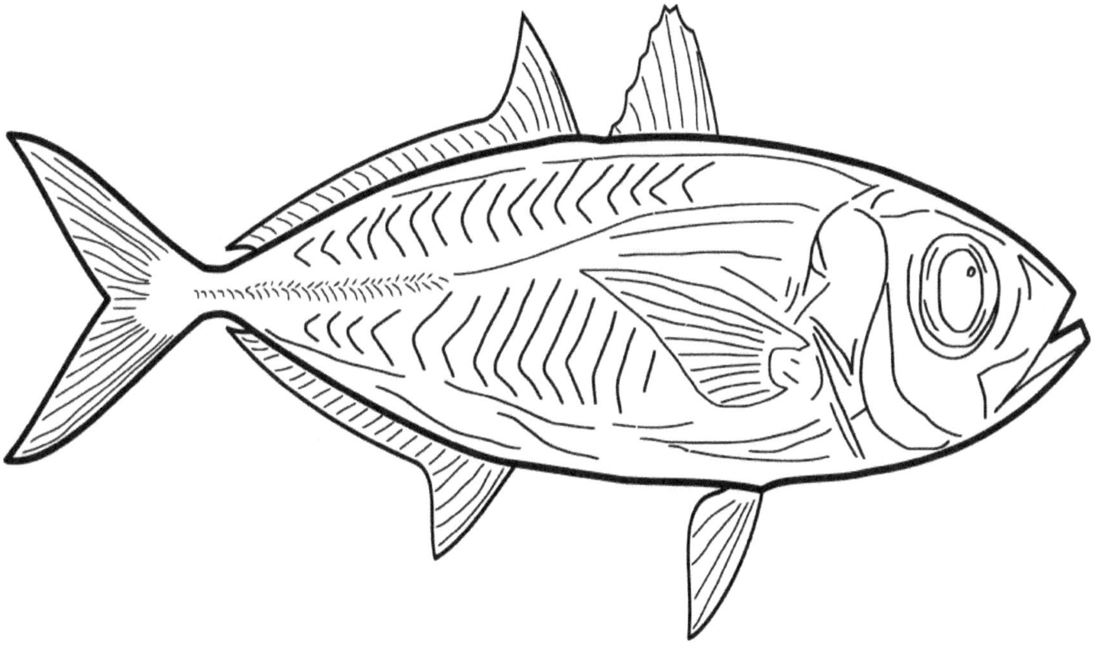

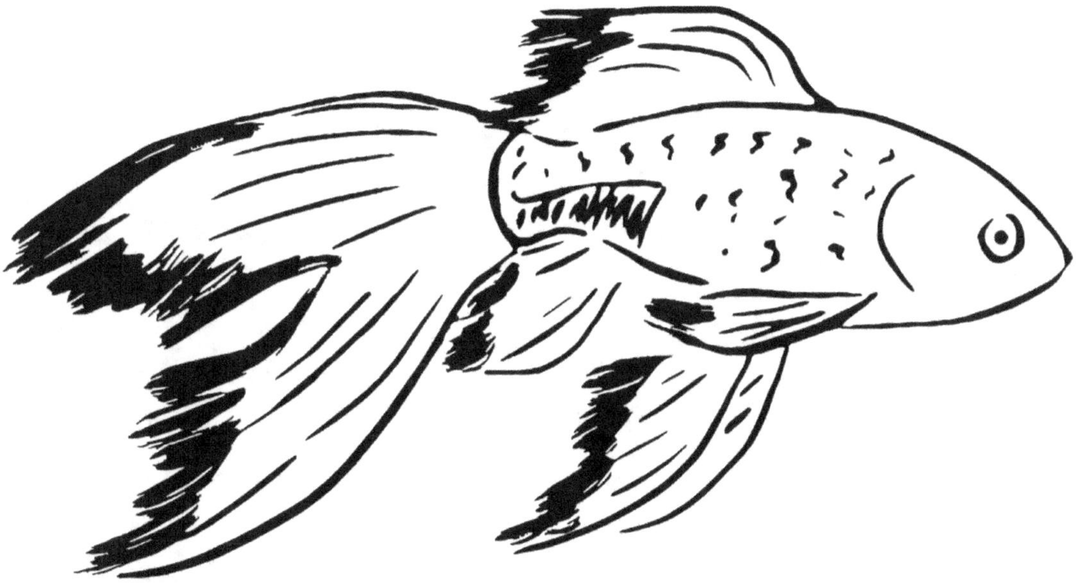

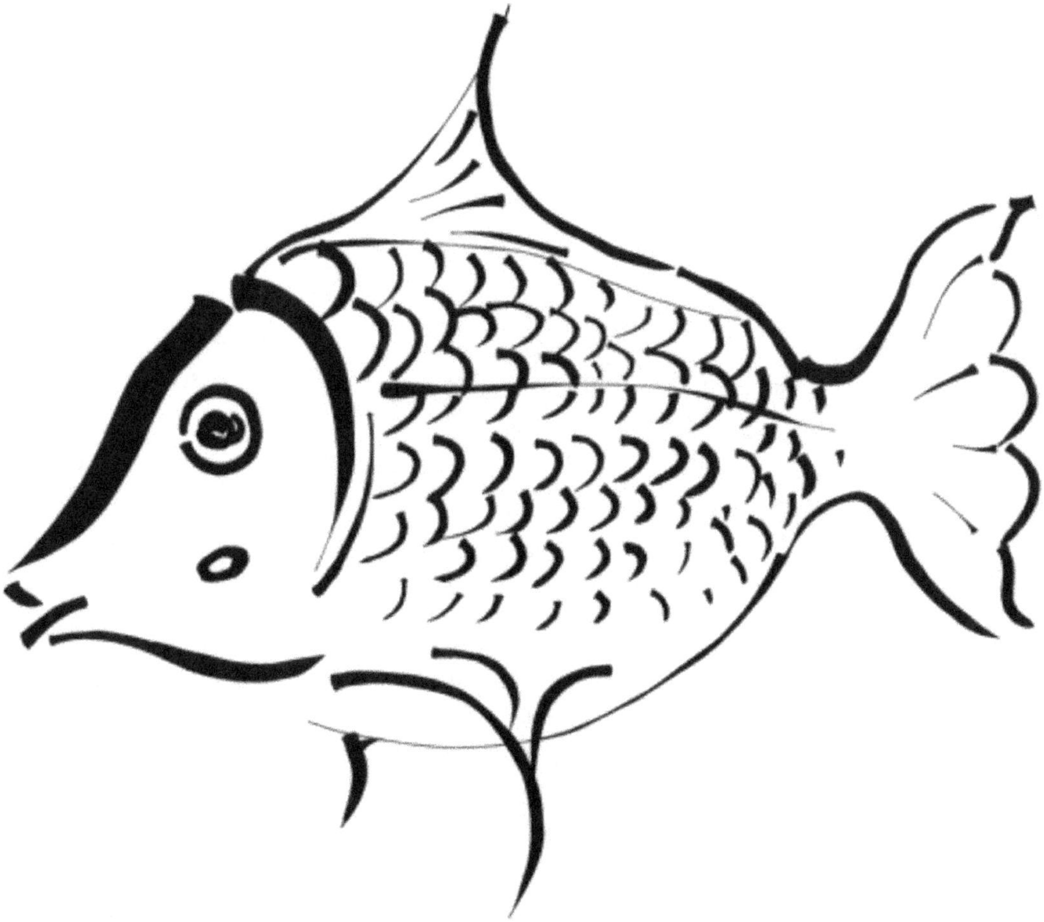

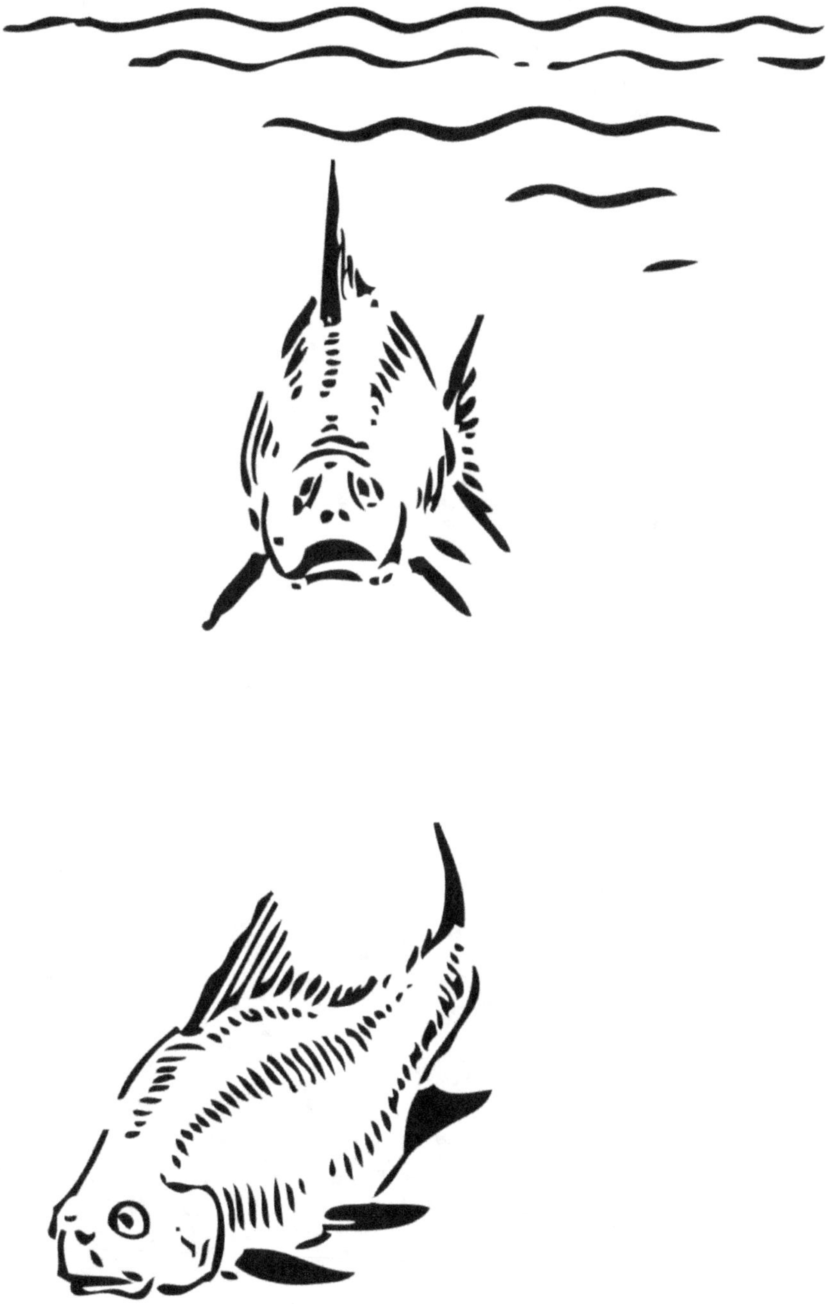

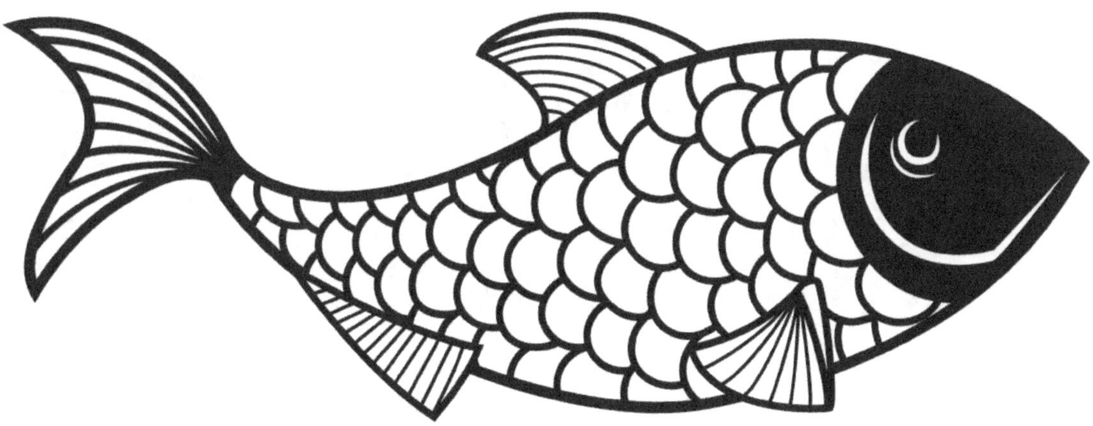

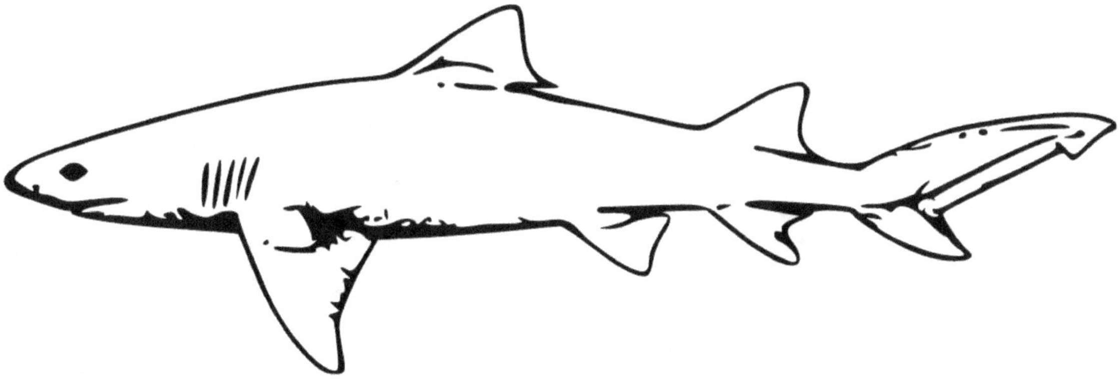

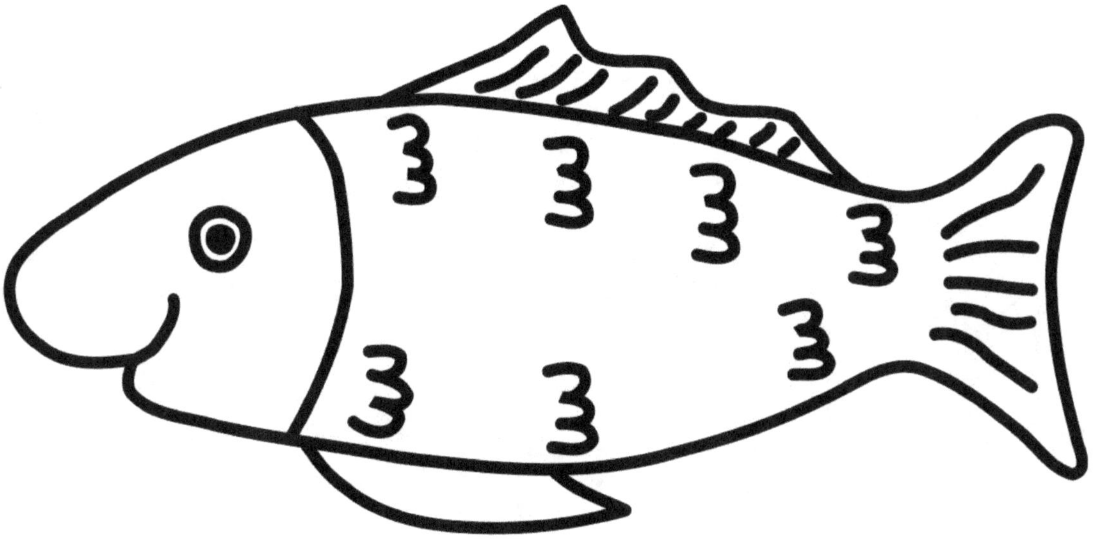

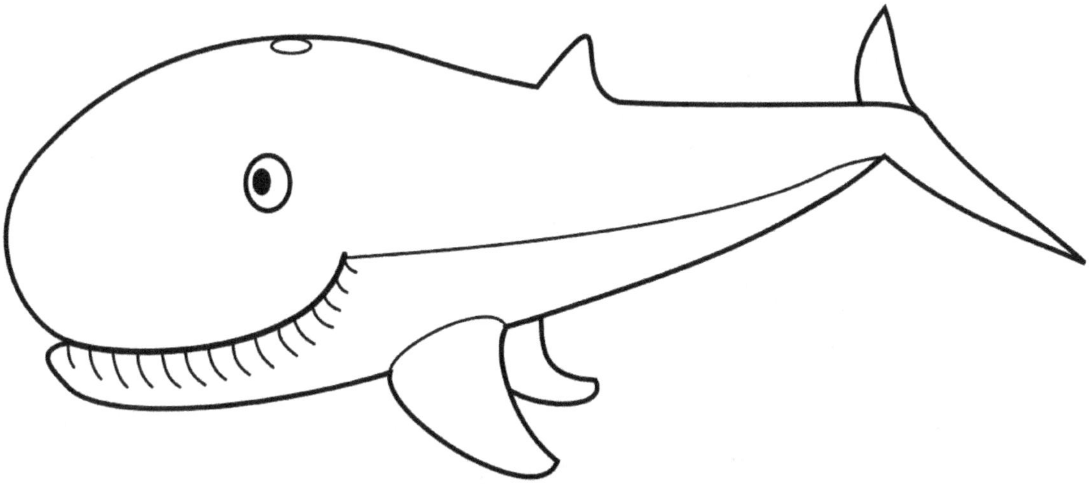